HOT AUGUST NIGHT/1970
THE FORGOTTEN LGBT RIOT

STEVEN F. DANSKY

Copyright © 2012 by Steven F. Dansky the author of this book. All rights reserved. The book author retains sole copyright to the contributions to this book.

ISBN-13:9780615596235

Photographs

Cover photographs and pages 4-5 by Richard Corkery, copyright © 2010 Daily News L.P.

Photograph pages 18-19, copyright © Diana Davies. "Gay "Be-In", Sheep Meadow, Central Park, New York, June 28, 1970." Reprinted with permission of Diana Davies Photographs, Manuscripts and Archives Division, The New York Public Library, Astor, Lenox and Tilden Foundations.

Photographs pages 30, 42, 45, 52-53, 72 by Steve Rose, *Come Out!*, Vol. 1, #5, August/September 1970.

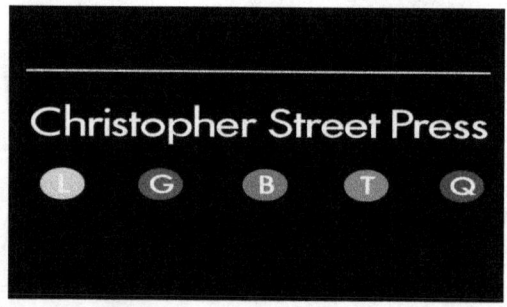

for
Bob Bland
(1947-2011)
and
Henry "Hank" Ferrari
(1951-1991)

Contributors

Steven F. Dansky	8
Bob Bland	25
Perry Brass	27
N.A. Diaman	29
Angela Douglas	35
Tim Elliott	39
Dana Gillespie	44
John Knoebel	47
Ken Lundgreen	55
Martha Shelley	61
Dennis Siple	66
Rich Wandel	68

Steven F. Dansky

Hot August Night/1970: The Forgotten LGBT Riot

1.

It is essential to historicize the lives of lesbians, gays, and transgendered people, because either we are marginalized, viewed through a heteronormative filter, or entirely hidden. For LGBT people, in particular, our life experiences are categorized by the distinctions of public-versus-private, personal-versus-political; rarely contextualized or traced along the long arc of macrohistory. Declarations of same-sex commitment and marriage are interpreted as personal occurrences, rather than as a political and public proclamation. The historical reconstruction requires crafting a narrative through memory and oral accounts. History is the art of memory. Memory is central to oral history-taking—it is pivotal; but, memory can be fragile subjective, unstable, and contingent on the different credibilities of interviewer and interviewee.

During the summer of 2011, I began an email correspondence with a historian who was writing about a cell that had at most, a handful of members that started in 1969 with Gay Liberation Front (GLF) New York, the first LGBT organization founded in direct response after the Stonewall Rebellion in New York.. GLF had many cells, small autonomous groups of individuals with a common purpose or ideology that operated independently from the organization. He was mystified after interviewing several of us about how to resolve our different memories of the cell—who founded the cell, in what month of what year, attended which meetings, or wrote what position papers. He said with exasperation, "How am I to make sense of these divergent memories." I told him, "Isn't that what historians do. That's your job."

Nevertheless, oral history-taking has its strengths and can be compelling. See "Act-Up Oral History Project," www.actuporalhistory.org; "Civil Rights Oral History Project," Birmingham Civil Rights Institute; "Documenting Lesbian Lives," Student Oral History Project, Smith College; "First Person Conversations with Holocaust Survivors," United States Holocaust Memorial Museum; or "Voices from the Days of

Slavery," Library of Congress. The Stonewall Rebellion is a case-in-point. Various accounts of the 1969 event, generally considered the demarcation from the homophile to the modern LGBT movement, the turning point and central event of the 20th century in LGBT history, entirely depend on the memory of those who self-declare to have been participants in the event. There are no other consistent or trustworthy accounts. Despite the inherent dilemmas of contested meanings, memory deficits, loss of resilience, the Rashomon effect, and political expediencies of oral or eye-witness accounts, a history of the event materialized. And the Stonewall Rebellion has been rendered in many works that have provided commanding first-hand accounts, such as Kate Davis and David Heilbroner's documentary *Stonewall Uprising*; and the books David Carter's *Stonewall: The Riots that Sparked the Gay Revolution*;" and "*Stonewall*," by Martin Duberman.

For several years since the 40th anniversary of GLF in 2009, many of the surviving members initiated a listserve and began email correspondences with each other. These renewed connections spread to other social networks, and many GLFers who were lost-to-contact for decades surfaced, as if from a Diaspora, from the rural provinces of Massachusetts, New York, Maine, and Ohio; to San Francisco, Philadelphia, and Portland; to Pahoa, Hawaii; to the southwest, Arizona and Nevada; the south, Florida and North Carolina; to other countries, Argentina, Australia, Mexico, Israel, Thailand; and to Fire Island, Greenwich Village, and the Haight-Ashbury. These correspondences have been catalytic as I reflected on those momentous events of the early LGBT movement. Continuously what soared in my consciousness was the Times Square demonstration on August 29, 1970 against police harassment and the subsequent riot that night in Greenwich Village. *Hot August Night/1970: The Forgotten LGBT Riot* emerged. This book is result of gathering testimony after the passing decades of those who were there. Below is mine.

2.

The dizzying momentum of 1968 was climactic with protests globally and in the United States. That year is comparable in this millennium to the start of the Occupy Movement in more than 95 cities across 82 countries; the 2011 Arab Awakening with revolutions in Tunisia, Egypt, Libya; civil uprisings in Bahrain, Syria, and Yemen with major protests in Algeria, Iraq, Jordan, Kuwait, Morocco and Oman. During 1968, hundreds-of-thousands demonstrated in the streets to protest the Vietnam War, forcing President Lyndon Johnson not to seek reelection. At Columbia University, thousands of students led a general strike to demand power in decision-making, and five buildings were occupied, causing a university shutdown. The Prague Spring saw the invasion of Czechoslovakia by 250,000 Warsaw Pact troops, mostly from the Soviet Union, violently suppressing political and cultural reforms. In Paris, 10 million workers began the most sustained general strike in France's history, threatening the very survival the Fifth Republic with President Charles de Gaulle fleeing to West Germany. In Mexico, more than 300 student demonstrators were killed by members of an elite presidential guard. The assassination of Martin Luther King, Jr., brought rebellion in Baltimore; Boston; Chicago; Cincinnati; Detroit; Washington, DC; Kansas City, Missouri; Nashville; Newark; New York; Pittsburgh; Trenton; and Oakland. Robert Kennedy was assassinated. *The New York Times* reported, "Miss America Pageant is Picketed by 100 Women. Women armed with a giant bathing beauty puppet and a 'freedom trash can' in which they threw girdles, bras, hair curlers, false eyelashes, and anything that smacked of 'enslavement' picketed the Miss America Pageant here today."

It was April 15, 1968. My twenty-fourth birthday. King was assassinated eleven days before. I was at a Lower East Side planning meeting for the Poor Peoples Campaign, which was to be King's protest to address economic injustice. I was going to Washington, DC, as part of the first-wave of demonstrators at Resurrection City, a complex of tents built on the National Mall.

That night, *Boys in the Band* opened Off-Broadway. Clive Barnes reviewed it in *The New York Times* writing, "The point is that is not a play about a homosexual, but a play that takes the homosexual milieu, and the homosexual way of life, totally for granted and uses this as a valid basis of human experience. "

3.

Below 14th was the great divide in Manhattan during the 1960s. It was a neighborhood distinct from the rest of New York City seemingly beyond the reach of gentrification. Artists migrated east from Greenwich Village after the apartment rents there became prohibitive, and they spray-painted psychedelia with the fluorescence of Day-Glo onto façades of early 20th century tenements built to warehouse immigrants.

I moved to New York City's Lower East Side. The address was 170 East 2nd Street, a former apartment of Allen Ginsberg, which I discovered seeing a photograph of him on a bedroom window sill. Michael Capizzi, my partner at the time, and I published a bilingual newsletter called *Peace/La Paz*. I wrote and typed articles onto stencils, placing them on a rotating cylinder of a manually operated mimeograph, squeezing ink from a tube, my hands blackened for days after printing hundreds of copies of the newsletter onto pastel-colored paper, then hand-collated, stapled, and hawked on the streets of Alphabet City from Avenue A to, charging a penny or giving them away.

It was June 29, 1969. I was fired as a substance-abuse counselor from Odyssey House, for being gay and unwilling to enter psychiatric treatment to cure my orientation.

That day, *The New York Times* reported, "hundreds of young men went on a rampage in Greenwich Village shortly after 3 am after a force of plainclothes men raided a bar that the police said was well known for its homosexual clientele."

A few days later, on July 2, 1969, *The Village Voice* declared, "Gay Power Comes to Sheridan Square. Full moon over the Stonewall."

4.

A month later in August 1969, I went to a meeting of Gay Liberation Front at Alternate U on 14th Street and 6th Avenue. The GLF meetings were always a hotbed of contention, something that many have documented in histories of the fledgling organization. The early movement attracted many LGBT people with antithetical political or apolitical viewpoints, not always reconcilable. By 1970, GLF was totally decentralized with more than nineteen cells, and I had been a member of no less than three, including Come Out! Newspaper; the Flaming Faggots; The Radical Study Group; and The Red Butterfly and; there were twelve consciousness raising groups, and I had been a member of no less than 3, such as Femmes Against Sexism; three communal households, and miscellaneous other caucuses that met on a regular basis. Then, as Emily Dickinson described, "If I feel physically as if the top of my head were taken off, I know that is poetry." I discovered feminism, and It all made sense at that precise moment of awareness. I helped found the Effeminist Movement.

It was June 28, 1970. The first pride march was a transformative event—the organizing principle, *out of the closet* realized as never before in history with thousands occupying the Sheep Meadow in Central Park. The next day, on June 29, 1970, *The New York Times*, interviewed Michael Brown, a GLF founder, who said, "We'll never have the freedom and civil rights we deserve as human beings unless we stop hiding in closets and in the shelter of anonymity."

5.

On August 29, 1970, four weeks after the first pride march in history, several members of the *Flaming Faggots*, a group I belonged to gathered to attend a demonstration in Times Square against police harassment. I always felt danger and vulnerability when attending GLF demonstrations—it wasn't the fear of being outed, but of being attacked by homophobic onlookers. A demonstration in Times Square was particularly audacious because we couldn't count on community support, as is the case in Greenwich Village. I remember circling 42nd Street from Broadway to 8th Avenue, marching past movie theaters, the Amsterdam, Apollo, Selwyn, and Empire, where I had cruised as a teenager, still living with my parents in the Bronx.

For decades, my memory of that hot August night in 1970 was encapsulated in "Homosexual Sonnets," a series of sonnets, some of which were written to me, by Kenneth Pitchford in *Color Photos of the Atrocities*, (Little, Brown).

> And then, our riot that August. Effeminate?
> Anger found the strength
>   in you (and strength is strength, beautiful, not to
> be confused
>   with the brutality by which those filthy sado-porn
> hucksters are pound
>   ing our movement into insignificance—for lots
> and lots of money), and the righteous strength to
>   topple the flowerpots of chic O'Henry's café
> with your graceful arms, amidst a crash of tables
>   chairs customers.

The sonnet seemed to say all that needed to be said. How a slight faggot, albeit ferocious, enraged by injustice, found courage, thinking nothing of the consequence of his actions, rioted through the night into morning alongside his comrades. A photograph of Pitchford full-face in the center of the melee made the *Daily News*.

6.

The aspiration and struggle of LGBT people is a cultural and political imperative, predictive of the future for everyone. Our quest for social justice, indeed our very survival, does not stand alone—rather, it is within a historical continuum that defines and directs the course for humanity, nonhumans, and the planet. In our history, there have solitary acts of rebellion: those rejections of victimization within our homophobic families, in the school yard, or in the battlefield. There are those instances of public acts of defiance that resulted in the 1973 declassification of homosexuality as a mental disorder by the American Psychiatric Association (APA); the 2003 Supreme Court decision in Lawrence v. Texas that overruled state's rights sodomy laws; the 2011 repeal of Don't Ask, Don't Tell (DADT) by President Obama's administration; and in 2012 the ongoing struggle for marriage equality with the legalization of same-sex marriage in Iowa, Connecticut, Massachusetts, New Hampshire, Vermont, and New York. There are those occurrences of direct, militant confrontation on the streets, in the communities where we live, speak, and assemble; such were the Stonewall and the August 1970 Rebellions.

When I solicited participants to contribute to *Hot August Night/1970*, several responded with the following. "What was the Times Square action about? I think I was there, but given the fact I probably went to 5-10 demos a week those days I have no recollection what that was about specifically." "I'd forgotten all about this, but once I read my own article I remembered writing it." "I don't remember an August 1970 riot. Who rioted?" "I have no recall of the riot."

But, from others, such as Bob Bland, "I do have strong, photographic memories of that event and the police torture that went on afterwards, even the court session." John Knoebel, "And this was the moment when the march became the riot. All pandemonium let loose. Sirens started howling as squad cars arrived and police tried to clear the streets." Martha Shelley, "Once again, the police stepped up their pre-election harassment of Village homosexuals; and once again, we struck back." Rich Wandel, "Foundation: a turning point, the beginning of all that came after, an important realization, made me part of a community."

Since the beginning of the modern LGBT movement last century, historians, archivists, and activists, among others, have uncovered many hundreds-of-thousands of tapes; photographs and snapshots; e-mail, postcard and letter correspondence; journals and Moleskin notebooks; and memorabilia, souvenirs, flyers, and political buttons. For more than a half-century, we have crafted a historiography in an effort to demonstrate how these fragments correlate with each other. Some are stored on hard-drives; in drawers; in temperature-and-humidity controlled, decentralized, individual archives; and in the neural connections throughout our collective brains. There is no Internet website that links to a centralized database, global information-sharing needs to be a LGBT movement priority. Many in the LGBT movement feel a sense of historical urgency to remember, record, give oral testimony, and archive.

In a 2012 email, Marc Schnapp, a former member of the Baltic Street Collective in Brooklyn, recollected about attending the 25th anniversary celebration of the Stonewall Rebellion in 1994.

> I remember seeing the amazing exhibition at the New York Public Library's, *Becoming Visible: The Legacy of Stonewall*. I was staring into a glass case with artifacts of the sort we kept stored in the basement our gay collective on Baltic Street (and that you and John [Knoebel] undoubtedly kept on the Lower East Side). A young man beside me struck up a conversation, and I found myself entering an oral-history narrative. I was thrilled to bear witness. I turned from the case and beheld the huge photomural of what must have been a GLF meeting at the Church of the Holy Apostles. I started to identify every face I could. But, then I lost my wind and felt faint. I realized suddenly that most of the men in that photo were gone. The young man asked if I was OK. I was. Just momentarily stunned. And even more certain about the importance of oral and visual narrative.

In Hannah Arendt's terms "to see historically and to think politically," the testimonies in *Hot August Night/1970* are a response to historical moments experienced during a period of political transformation. An early definition of the word history is the relation of incidents whether true or imaginary—only later did the definition come to mean events professedly true. Later historians will sift through these memories, accurate, misremembered, or disremembered, past political crosscurrents and self-interest. Those historians will make sense of our story; make it known, after we're all gone.

Flyer for GLF Dance, July 31, 1970. Courtesy of John Knoebel.

¡ EL ASUNTO ESTÁ CALIETE!!

DEMOSTREMOS PARA TERMINAR EL HOSTIGAMIENTO A LA GENTE HOMOSEXUAL EN LA CALLE 42.

300 HOMOSEXUALES FUERON ARRESTADOS ALLÍ EN LAS ÚLTIMAS DOS SEMANAS.

LA 3RD AVENIDA Y LOS RAMBLES (EN CENTRAL PARK) FUERON OCUPADOS POR LA JARA LE ULTIMA SEMANA.

LOS CERDOS ESTÁN OCUPANDO TODOS LOS CENTROS HOMOSEXUALES DE LA CIUDAS.

Y EL VILLAGE SERÁ EL SIGUIENTE!!

¡ SALGAN!!

SÁBADO A LA NOCHE
29 DE AGOSTO, 8:30 P. M.

NOS ENCONTRAMOS EN LA ESQUINA SUDOESTE DE LA 8TH AVE. Y 42ND ST. (AL LADO DE LA PLAYA DE ESTACIONAMIENTO). TRAIGAN CARTELONES, BANDERAS, ENSEÑAS PARA PICKETEAR.

THE HEAT'S ON!!

DEMONSTRATE TO END POLICE HARASSMENT OF GAYS ON 42ND STREET.

300 GAYS BUSTED THERE IN THE LAST TWO WEEKS.

3RD AVE. & THE RAMBLES RAIDED LAST WEEK.

PIGS ARE RAIDING EVERY GAY CENTER IN THE CITY---

THE VILLAGE IS NEXT!!.

COME OUT!!

SATURDAY NITE
AUGUST 29TH, 8:30 P.M.

MEET ON SOUTHWEST CORNER OF 8TH AVE. & 42ND ST.(AT PARKING LOT). BRING BANNERS, FLAGS, SIGNS, FOR PICKETING.

Flyer for Times Square Demonstration, 1970.
Courtesy of John Knoebel.

Photograph copyright © Diana Davies. "Gay "Be-In", Sheep Meadow, Central Park, New York, June 28, 1970." Reprinted with permission of Diana Davies Photographs, Manuscripts and Archives Division, The New York Public Library, Astor, Lenox and Tilden Foundations.

Protest March by Homosexuals Sparks Disturbance in 'Village'

By FRANK J. PRIAL

Several hundred youths roamed through Greenwich Village streets last night and early this morning after a demonstration by homosexual organizations ended. They smashed windows in at least two stores, set several minor fires and overturned two automobiles.

The demonstration by the homosexual groups began around 9 P.M. near Times Square with about 250 placard-carrying and slogan-shouting young men and women parading on the sidewalk along 42d Street to protest alleged police harassment of homosexuals in the Times Square area recently.

Later the group marched downtown, stopping outside the 14th Precinct in West 35th Street before proceeding down Seventh Avenue to Sheridan Square in Greenwich Village.

The demonstration and march, sponsored by the Gay Liberation Front and the Gay Activists' Alliance, was without incident until the group broke up just before midnight at Sheridan Square.

Then, according to the police, some of the demonstrators joined with passersby and some of the usual large Saturday night throng in the Village to march around the Women's House of Detention at Greenwich Avenue and the Avenue of the Americas.

When the police attempted to break up the later demonstration the youths ran in several directions.

Others went west in Christopher Street where they overturned two automobiles, set trash-can fires in Sheridan Square Park, smashed the windows of a shop at 45 Christopher Street, and apparently turned in a false fire alarm.

The police at the Charles Street station said at least 10 youths had been detained on a variety of charges.

The New York Times, August 30, 1970

Protest March by Homosexuals Sparks Disturbance in 'Village'

Several hundred youths roamed through Greenwich Village Streets last night and early this morning after a demonstration by homosexual organizations ended. They smashed windows in at least two stores, set several minor fires and overturned two automobiles.

The demonstration by the homosexual groups began around 9 P.M. near Times Square with about 250 placard-carrying and slogan-shouting young men and women parading on the sidewalk along 42nd Street to protest alleged police harassment of homosexuals in the Times Square area recently.

Later the group marched downtown, stopping outside the 14th Precinct in West 35th Street before proceeding down Seventh Avenue to Sheridan Square in Greenwich Village.

The demonstration and march, sponsored by the Gay Liberation Front and the Gay Activists' Alliance, was without incident until the group broke up just before midnight at Sheridan Square.

Then, according to the police, some of the demonstrators joined with passersby and some of the usual large Saturday night throng in the Village to march around the Women's House of Detention at Greenwich Avenue and the Avenue of the Americas.

When the police attempted to break up the later demonstration the youths ran in several directions.

Others went west in Christopher Street where they overturned two automobiles, set trash-can fires in Sheridan Square, smashed the windows of a shop at 45 Christopher Street, and apparently turned in a false fire alarm.

The police at the Charles Street station said at least 10 youths had been detained on a variety of charges.

Gay Lib Parade, Riot in Village

A parade of some 350 homosexuals, members of the Gay Activists Alliance and the Gay Liberation Front, paraded on W. 42d St. Saturday night. Carrying signs, shouting demands, singing and clapping, they marched from Times Square to Greenwich Village, where a demonstration took place outside the Women's House of Detention, Sixth Ave. and 10th St. In ensuing ruckus, seven cops were hurt, including one knifed, and 18 arrests were made.

Carrying signs, clapping and waving, gay libs parade.

Demonstrators find discretion better part of valor as they flee scene of melee at Sixth Ave. and 10th St.

Photo caption above: "Carrying signs, clapping and waving, gay libs parade."
Photo caption below: "Demonstrators find discretion better part of valor as they flee scene of melee at Sixth Avenue and 10th St. "

New York Daily News, August 30, 1970

"Gay Lib Parade Riot in Village"

A parade of some 350 homosexuals, members of the Gay Activists Alliance and the Gay Liberation Front, parade on W. 42nd Street Saturday night. Carrying signs and clapping, they marched from Times to Greenwich Village where a demonstration took place outside the Women's House of Detention, Sixth Avenue, and 10th St. In ensuing ruckus, seven cops were hurt, including one knifed, and 18 arrests were made.

Bob Bland
(1947-2011)

I remember the House of D "riot" quite well since I was arrested and taken to the dungeon of the police station on 12th street.

We had marched up 6th Avenue and then back down, where we were blocking the Christopher/6th intersection. We were shouting slogans in favor of the incarcerated women when the police decided to clear us out. We saw someone being beaten that we thought was Giles Kotcher. Ken Lundgreen went ballistic and did a flying kick that landed on the leader of the police. Ken landed on his back and I somehow was able to grab him and toss the 6'4" Ken out of the range of police. I was in high heels at the time and unable to run fast enough to elude the police myself.

I was handcuffed in the dungeon next to the person who we had thought was Giles Kotcher. He had apparently hit a policeman and was sadistically beaten through the night. Kicked in the balls and hit in the face. I was threatened with the same treatment if I did not disclose the identity of the person I had rescued. I upped my masochism level and refused repeatedly, looking my interrogator in the eyes and lying. Somehow, I gained his respect for that and he never did beat me.

Sometime in the wee hours of the night, a lawyer from the National Lawyers Guild arrived and I was released. Later, in court, the charges were not pressed or whatever the right legal term is. I'm not sure what happened to the person handcuffed next to me, who turned out to be a (supposedly) straight anarchist.

From 1970-71, Bob Bland was a member of Gay Liberation Front and the 17th Street Collective.

Perry Brass

I remember this demonstration and the aftermath on 8th Street & 6th very well. We did a photo layout about in the next issue of *Come Out!* that had a picture of Hank Ferrari, and pictures of us, and of the cops. I was with my friend Tom Finley at the demo in Times Square & I do remember the march downtown to the Village—the sheer adrenaline of it made the trip downtown seem like it lasted about 10 minutes. What I remember, with crystal clarity, was Bob Bland doing this totally fantastic jack-knife kick right into a cop's face (or some other part of him). I was totally thrilled. I'm not sure if Bob remembers it, or wants to. That he was arrested was also part of my memory.

Poet, novelist, and activist, Perry Brass has been involved with the LGBT movement since 1969; he has published sixteen books. His latest is *King of Angels, A Novel About the Genesis of Identity and Belief*. His previous book was *The Manly Art of Seduction*; he can be reached at www.perrybrass.com (http://www.perrybrass.com) .

N. A. Diaman

Greenwich Village in Flames

I volunteered to be a monitor for a Times Square demonstration to protest police harassment of Midtown Manhattan gays. It was was cosponsored by Gay Liberation Front (GLF) and Gay Activists Alliance (GAA). In preparation, I attended an afternoon workshop in nonviolent tactics and was given an armband to wear at the demonstration.

The Saturday night demonstration was peaceful and orderly, but militant. The demonstrators marched single file in a circle, carrying placards and chanting outside the theaters, arcades, fast-food joints, and cheap hotels on 42nd Street. After an hour, someone suggested we go to the local precinct station to voice our demand that the police stop their harassment and indiscriminate arrests of gays. "To Greenwich Village!" Someone shouted after a few minutes outside the police station. We slowly made our way southward as a group of about hundred women and men, along a deserted avenue, passing nondescript brick buildings and empty lots. En route, someone was injured by an empty beer bottle hurled from a roof or upper floor of a building.

We walked the mile-and-half distance, stopping outside the Women's House of Detention, a women's prison from 1932 to 1974 at 10 Greenwich Avenue, known colloquially as the *House of D.* It had windows facing the street, giving the women inmates the opportunity to communicate with passersby. We chanted raucously, "Free our sisters! Free our sisters!" No doubt, some of the incarcerated prisoners were lesbians. And they responded from the top floor, calling down to us. It was difficult to tell what was happening inside the building, but evidently a commotion was developing. Then, a length of toilet paper was ignited, hurled from a window it floated toward the street, the flaming paper flickered down.

We moved westward along Christopher Street, startled to find the police were about to raid a gay bar at One Sheridan Square. They expected many LGBT people would've been preoccupied with the Times Square demonstration. They didn't welcome the presence of a large group of angry protesters. The police charged head-on, forcefully pushing us back. They demanded that we immediately clear the streets and move onto the sidewalk. It happened suddenly--I wasn't prepared or fast enough to avoid a policeman clubbing me. I was distracted from the raid of the gay bar—my immediate concern was to protect myself from further violence.

I turned back toward Sixth Avenue and spent the next couple of hours near Eighth Street, watching an incredible riot erupt. I saw bottles thrown and windows smashed. The police were brutal: clubbing individuals and dragging them away. I was transfixed and in a state of shock. Another GLF member advised me to remove my armband so as not to be an easy target for the police during the melee.

I saw people I knew who were battling with the police, running from the scene both on Sixth Avenue and the first block of Eighth Street. Then a very dramatic moment occurred. From the sidelines, I witnessed Hank Ferrari—an active and militant GLFer—kneel in a pool of blood. In a spontaneous gesture of rage he smeared it on his face. And he shouted, "This is the blood of my gay brothers!"

Later that evening someone went to the Sixth Precinct to get a list of those arrested so GLF could post bail. Profits from GLF dances were used to pay bail for gay people regardless of the charges against them. It was another of the services we provided to the community. I was in the courtroom the following morning along with several other GLF members to make certain everyone arrested during the riot was released.

Newspaper reporters and some GAA leaders publicly blamed GLF for the riot, which I thought was unfair since I distinctly remember one of them urging demonstrators to march back to the Village, referring to it as our "home turf." Once the police charged the crowd, no individual or group of people from either organization orchestrated what occurred. GLF called a press conference at the Church of the Holy Apostles, where GLF held its weekly meetings, to refute allegations made by GAA. Four or five lesbians and gay men representing GLF agreed to answer questions on the condition that no photographs be taken because some of them weren't out publicly. But, as soon as the ten or twelve reporters began asking questions, they brought out their cameras and started taking photos indiscriminately. Activists and journalists shouted at each other.

I crawled along the floor following the electrical cables to the power outlets in the room, yanking out whatever I could from the wall before running downstairs to look for the circuit box. Along the way I passed a gay wedding being performed in the chapel. A few moments later I pulled the switch that plunged the entire building into darkness, angering both wedding party and press, but allowing my closeted gay sisters and brothers the opportunity to escape.

N. A Diaman is the author of ten books published by Persona Press. The last four titles are: *The City* (a novel), *Following My Heart* (a memoir) and two travel memoirs: *Paris Dreams* and *Athens Apartment*. For more information see www.nikosdiaman.com

Photograph © copyright 1970 by Steve Rose.

Angela Douglas
(1943-2007)

GAYS, STRAIGHTS UNITE TO FIGHT MISS BASH

Raising the orange and black banner of the Gay Liberation Front of New York and the blue and gold banner of the Gay Activists Alliance high in proud defiance of police orders that no banners could be carried, around 200 gays marched to protest fascist harassment and the arrests of over 300 gays in the 42nd street area during the past several weeks.

Several Black Panthers marched with the group for a short distance.

After circling 42nd street several times, closely guraded by dozens of police, the gays continued the march to the nearest police station, shouting "end police harassment" and "off the pig."

The march then continued to the Christopher street area of Greenwich village. Enroute, several gays were injured from missiles thrown from skyscapers.

Upon reaching the women's huse of detention, which is at the corner where Christopher street begins, the gays met several thousand people who had come out of curiosity and to give support. Hundreds more came as word spread. The women in the prison rioted and set fire to several cells, threw trash on fire from the windows. Gays continued the march, their ranks swelled by hundreds, down Christopher street to Sheridan sqaure sections of and tore down the iron fence surrounding it. Then the march went on to a unisex club which had just been raided, called the Haven. During the protest outside of the Haven, police attacked and the group retreated.

Gays, Straights Unite to Fight Miss Bash

Raising the orange and black banner of the Gay Liberation Front of New York and the blue and gold banner of the Gay Activists Alliance high in proud defiance of police orders that no banners could be carried, around 200 gays marched to protest fascist harassment and the arrests of over 300 gays in the 42nd street area during the past several weeks.

Several Black Panthers marched with the group for a short distance.

After circling 42nd Street several times, closely guarded by dozens of police, the gays continued the march to the nearest police station, shouting "end police harassment" and "off the pig."

The march then continued to the Christopher Street area of Greenwich Village. En route, several gays were injured from missiles thrown from skyscrapers.

Upon reaching the Women's House of Detention, which is at the corner where Christopher Street begins, the gays met several thousand people who had come out of curiosity and to give support. Hundreds more came as word spread. The women in the prison rioted and set fire to several cells, threw trash on fire from the windows. Gays continued the march; their ranks swelled by hundreds, down Christopher Street to Sheridan Square and tore down sections of the iron fence surrounding it. Then the march went on to a unisex club which had just been raided, called the Haven. During the protest outside of the Haven, police attacked and the group retreated.

By this time, a large crowd had completely filled 8th Street, and the gays sat down refusing to comply with police orders to disperse. Undercover police attempted to disperse the crowd by claiming they were gay leaders.

Police attacked again, brutally beating one young man, splashing large quantities of blood from head wounds onto the street.

Outraged people retaliated with rocks and bottles. After this skirmish, people wiped up the blood and painted their faces with it. A man with a gun, not police apparently, was seen on a roof and police ran like hell.

Hundreds of tactical police arrived and attacked the crowd several times, but after each assault, the people would reassemble and hurl missiles at them. Gays reassembled on Christopher Street, overturned several cars, and were attacked again by police. Several gunshots were heard.

The rioting was continuing at three a.m. According to rather incomplete information, at least six people were seriously beaten, one possibly dead; no estimate of number of arrests. One undercover policeman wounded by a savage kick when he attempted to arrest a freedom fighter; no looting. Several vehicles damaged.

At the beginning of the march, someone ripped off a restaurant across the street from the assembly point while police stood around to make sure no sexual crimes were committed.

The previous evening, around 150 gays demonstrated at New York University to protest the school's halting of all-gay dances. After several hours of picketing, school officials gave in and opened the doors. A victory dance was held. About three a.m. the following morning, two gays (male) were hospitalized after being attacked by a band of about twenty club-wielding straights. The Haven had been raided, also, and about 500 people were in the area. A group of about 50 armed gay males secured the area from the bigots.

Apparently the group of male heterosexuals, who were young, swept Christopher Street, attacking gays at random.

More gay power demonstrations are planned, including a protest against the firing of a lesbian who marched in the massive Women's Liberation Day march on August 26, [1970], carrying a banner reading "lesbians unite."

The second Christopher Street rebellion was the first time that gays and straights united to fight a common oppressor, appropriately called "Miss Bash" by gays. Shouting "gay power" and "power to the people," gays and straights let the fascists know very clearly that the streets belong to all the people.

All power to gay people. All power to all the people.

On August 29 and the morning of August 30, the people were over three thousand strong on Christopher Street.

Angela Douglas, a contentious yet effective advocate of transgender rights was a member of GLF, New York and Los Angeles. In 1970, she founded Transsexual/Transvestite Action Organization), which published the *Moonshadow* and *Mirage* newsletters.

Tim Elliott

We were shouting the slogans, "Gay is Good," and "Gay Power"

I don't know if it was the first Gay Pride March on June 28, 1970 that set off the New York City police or not, but in August of that year they went on a rampage raiding gay bars in the city. They'd gotten away with it without incident until June 1969 when as they were raiding the Stonewall Inn, much to their surprise, gays and lesbians fought back. Even more shocking to them was the fact that most of the ones in that bar who did the fighting back were drag queens, the very ones the police least expected to resist a raid. So, when the first anniversary of that event turned into what seemed to those of us involved, a major success, the first annual Gay Pride March, perhaps the police decided to show us who was boss by raiding several of our bars two months later.

A joint march was planned by both GLF members and GAA members in opposition to these raids and it took place on a dog-day night in late August. We were emboldened by the extreme success of the march in June. Some incidents had occurred shortly before that earlier march where a few of my friends had been viciously attacked in the village simply because they were gay. But much to our surprise, the Gay Pride March itself was peaceful and the huge crowd that congregated in the Sheep's Meadow on that day at the end of the march might as well have been a million to us who were there. We joined the crowds that first anniversary not knowing what was going to happen to us and when we actually weren't killed, it made joining this second march in August much easier.

My lover and I were members of that demonstration that August night in 1970, and as we were shouting the slogans, "Gay is Good", "Gay Power", and other affirming statements with our gay and lesbian brothers and sisters, the two of us marched down Seventh Avenue from Times Square to the West Village with our arms around the other's shoulders.

We noticed this one policeman was watching the two of us intently. Most certainly, he had never seen two men being that affectionate with one another and it seemed to bother him in some personal way as if we were an affront to him particularly. When we arrived in the Village, tempers began to flare between the marchers and the police and when that one policeman that had been watching my lover and I the whole route saw that the situation was beginning to deteriorate, he raced toward the two of us with his "billy club" raised high. His intent was to bash the two of our heads in, but another policeman with a cooler head, stopped him just in the nick of time before he sent the two of us sprawling on the pavement drenched in blood.

Only a few minutes later, violence did erupt and it was not only those in the march that found themselves as recipients of the police anger, but those on the sidelines watching the action also got pulled into the mayhem as well. On that scorching hot night in August, the police seemed to be determined to make someone pay and it didn't really matter much to them who it was.

The violence seemed to last forever and the main image that still sticks in my mind about that event is that of a young blond man being pulled off the sidewalk and being drug by a policeman by the hair across the street and the policeman was beating him relentlessly with his "billy club". Heads were really being bashed in and my lover and I looked at each other with the realization that if that policeman with the calmer temperament hadn't stepped in earlier, it would have been us who was having our blood spilled as well.

I've long since forgiven those policeman who spilled blood that night, even the one who wanted to spill the blood of my lover and I before he was stopped. I've learned that all of us can only know what we have been taught. What everyone in American society had been taught who were at that march that night was to hate gays and lesbians even those of us who were gay and lesbian. We were for the first time in our lives beginning to love ourselves if even only a little and it was more than the New York City Police could take so they struck out at us.

Thank goodness the violent demonstrations like the one in August of 1970 were few and far between because I don't believe now that violent revolution works. The only revolutions that are lasting are the ones that are achieved non-violently. Revolution did occur in the gay and lesbian community all over America and I'm thrilled that I'm still here to help tell about it. I most likely would not have been here now if the revolution had turned violent.

Tim Elliott was born and raised in North Carolina and lived in New York City from 1968 to 1973. He was there for the beginning of the modern Gay Liberation Movement and he's glad.

Photograph © copyright 1970 by Steve Rose.

Dana Gillespie

I wasn't at the Times Square end, but Billy Weaver and I were involved at the village end, particularly the fighting & rioting that night on Christopher Street and West 8th Street.

We never intended to get into trouble—all the fighting on the streets came as a surprise to both of us.

We were outside the Women's House of D while burning sheets, and more came flying out from between the bars on upstairs windows.

That was the night Billy was arrested on Christopher (he was standing right next to me when the cops grabbed him and whisked him away.

After he spent a night in the Tombs, I bailed Billy out.

I spent an interesting day in court-- there were lots of people there, all picked up in the village during the previous evening's melee.

It was quite a night-- a Saturday night, as I recall.

I don't know of any official accounts, but I was there, with Billy Weaver, for the worst of it.

Billy was arrested that night, and I have vivid memories of what we went through.

The few mentions I've ever seen referred to it as "brief"—but as far as we were concerned, it was heavy duty stuff.

And as far as photos go—I didn't see any cameras that night, and I don't recall any media being there, either.

Dana Gillespie was a member of the Gay Liberation Front.

Photograph © copyright 1970 by Steve Rose.

John Knoebel

An Expression of Gay Rage: The August 1970 Village Riot

I missed the Stonewall Riot completely—only arriving in New York to attend graduate school a week after it was over. But by the summer of 1970, I'd been a full-time activist with the Gay Liberation Front (GLF) for over 9 months, attending meetings, participating in numerous demonstrations, the first Gay Pride March and so much more. With five other men from GLF, I was living in the West 95th Street Collective. The August 1970 March and Village Riot remains one of my most vivid memories of that summer in New York.

I recall it all started like this. In late July of 1970, several young Hispanic gay men came to a regular Sunday night GLF meeting at the Church of the Holy Apostle on 9th Ave to talk about an ongoing police clean-up of Times Square. They reported a serious situation in which many young gay men and lesbians were being rounded up and hauled off to jail on trumped up charges. I think few GLFers were familiar with the Times Square gay scene or had spent much time in the mid-town 42nd street area, but we all knew there was a large gay minority presence in the Times Square area that was historically as long-standing as the East and West Village gay scenes that most GLF members belonged to. Two of the men who spoke in semi-drag at the meeting that night said that they had merely been standing in line at a movie theater when they were approached, roughed up and arrested by police. The word was that the city wanted to get rid of the gay presence on 42nd Street and they said that dozens, if not hundreds, of such phony arrests had been made on recent Saturday and Sunday nights. Couldn't we do something?

Over the next few minutes, speakers around the room responded. How about organizing a protest march? How about calling the other gay groups, Gay Activists Alliance (GAA), Radicalesbians, Street Transvestite Action Revolutionaries (STAR), and do a joint march in Times Square on an upcoming Saturday night? A consensus was formed. Did the chairperson of the month clomp the bat on the floor? Who remembers, but the idea received enthusiastic support. In the next few days, there was an organizing meeting that brought gay groups together and formalized plans for a protest march in Times Square for Saturday night, August 29th. I didn't attend, but two of my roommates in my 95th Street Living Collective went and volunteered us to be monitors for the march. There started to be a lot of talk. GAA was on board, too. Flyers got posted in the Village. *Assemble next Saturday night at 8:30pm at the parking lot on the SW corner of 8th Ave. and 42nd street. Bring banners, flags and signs for picketing.* The plan was to march for an hour or so, then lead the march to the local 14th Precinct Police Station on 35th St. bet 8th and 9th Avenues and conclude with a protest there.

Several hundred of us descended on Times Square that night. It was an amazing turn out. I think few of us were prepared for the actual scene on 42nd Street. This was long before the "Disneyfication" of Times Square into today's tourist friendly mecca. Despite the presence of the legitimate Broadway theaters and movie palaces, the area was frankly run down and seedy, filled with bars, adult shops and porn theaters. Hot August weather had brought out the crowds. Pedestrians were so thick all along 42nd Street that it was hard to see how we could have a successful march. But as the line of march took shape, we set off marching and yelling down the sidewalk to Broadway and 7th Avenue, across the street, back up to 8th Avenue, across the street, round and round we went. People stood back and let us pass. So many marchers were there that we seemed to fill the sidewalks on both sides of 42nd Street in a continuous running circle. It was thrilling, yet there was a feeling of danger in the air. Our signs read "Gay Power" and "Stop Police Brutality." Many in the crowd on the streets smiled and cheered us, but others looked decidedly hostile. There was a sense of pushing. When the traffic lights started changing on busy 42nd Street, we ran to cross the street with the rest of the marchers so as not be left behind. The lights of the signs and porn theater marquise were bright as daylight. Police presence was all around us, but no one interfered with the march. After 30 to 45 minutes, it was enough and the call went out to move onto the precinct station.

As monitors, we five members of the 95th Street Living Collective found ourselves at the head of the march and walking alongside the very first section of marchers. Heading south down 8th Avenue brought a complete change of scene. We left behind the bright lights of 42nd Street and entered into the practically deserted streets of the West 30s. The marchers stayed in line, but quieted down completely, feeling good about the adrenalin rush of the past 45 minutes. As we turned onto 35th Street, however, it was clear that a mistake had been made in planning to conclude the demonstration at the Midtown South Precinct. Down the street right in front of the precinct station stood about 20 to 30 helmeted policemen, lined up across the street, each with a Billy club waiting for us. No pedestrians were around at all. It must have been around 11pm. We halted the march and two from the 95th Street Collective, David Lasky and Larry Kovacs, and I had a quick huddle. What do we do with all these marchers? No way were we going to lead them into the certain violent confrontation waiting ahead of us. Then it occurred to us. Let's go on to the Village. It seemed the only and best idea. So we turned and started shouting "To the Village, to the Village!" The chant was taken up down the line and with one accord the entire line of the march turned and started back down 35th Street. to $8t^h$ Avenue.

Within minutes we bunched out onto the street, stopping traffic, chanting, heading to home turf. It seemed to take no time at all and we were south of 14th Street again. We turned down Greenwich Avenue towards 7th Avenue and Christopher Street. "Join Us! Join us!" rang out. For what? To do what? Who knew, but the surge was unstoppable. It was a hot night in the Village. Almost immediately it seemed that our numbers swelled tenfold. The bars emptied. Hundreds of people just started shouting. "Gay Power! Gay Power Now!" Then the march was fully overwhelmed by the size of the crowd and ceased to exist. This was the moment when the march became the riot. All pandemonium let loose. Sirens started howling as squad cars arrived and police tried to clear the streets. But all in vain. The crowd surged. Trash baskets flew at the police. Bottles filled the air. The whole area from Greenwich Avenue to Sheridan Square was a sea of bodies. "Gay Power, Gay Power." A generation of gays and lesbians declared that change had come. At the Women's House of Detention at 6th Avenue and Greenwich Avenue, female prisoners were screaming and calling down encouragement from their cell windows, dropping lighted pieces of paper that fluttered down in flames onto the street below. We shouted up at them, "Hey! Hey!, Ho! Ho! House of D. has got to go!"

Just across the way, Eighth Street. east of 6th Avenue was closed to traffic on weekend summer nights to become a pedestrian mall and so it immediately filled with the overflow from narrow Christopher Street. Here's where some of the worst damage occurred. Store windows were smashed, cars overturned, trash cans were set on fire. Police clubbed people in the crowd and hauled others away. GLFer Hank Ferrari stooped and covered his hands in blood from the street, then rubbed it all over his face, shouting "We must avenge the blood of our brothers!" Those who saw him will always remember the expression of gay rage on his face.

For my own part, I stayed for a time in the Sheridan Square area, chanting arm and arm with the others from my Collective, surging this way and that with the force of the crowd. Then I got struck on the hand by a stray thrown bottle and joined others in St. Vincent's Hospital emergency room waiting hours for x-rays and stitches. Many others were arrested. Disturbances continued into the wee hours of Sunday morning and continued on for two more nights, though not so big and with a lot less gay participation. I recall pretty good coverage in the next day's newspapers. We'd shaken up New York City again! On Monday or Tuesday, I remember holding the bail money with fellow GLFer Bob Kohler at the courthouse downtown when our friends' cases came up.

John Knoebel, a senior executive with *The Advocate* for over three decades whose writing on gay history and politics have appeared in numerous books and magazines, was an early gay activist in Gay Liberation Front in 1969. He advocated a close affinity between gay liberation and radical feminism as a founder of the New York Effeminists through their publication, *Double-F:A Magazine of Effeminism*.

Photograph © copyright 1970 by Steve Rose.

Ken "Spinstar" Lundgreen

Bob Bland acted as the original draft producer of The Gay Revolution manifestos. I did not know he was dead. I've shut myself off from past associations & have otherwise been out of touch for some years now. I'm afraid I'm in such poor condition at the moment & for anytime in the foreseeable future as to make rendering a detailed account too much of a time consuming challenge.

I was chosen to mark the lead of the 42nd street protest at a planning meeting convened at 17th St Collective for my height & long blonde hair being easily spotted from well back in the demo at night. We conformed to police demands to form a single or double file picket. Our sudden march on the Precinct was turned to a march-by when I decided to obey the event commander's direction to turn away at the end of that block which felt like a pointlessly defenseless trap with all the lights turned off before we arrived. I was remiss in not ensuring the march stayed together & only found out days later that someone was struck with a rock from a construction site & had to leave for the hospital. The march was dissipated & mostly over by the time we ran up to the front door of the Women's House of Detention & began pounding & demanding to let them go before hearing that the police were raiding the Gay Bar across the street from where the Stonewall was. As we approached a very large & aggressive police presence burst from there & seemingly otherwise nowhere driving us back on the sidewalk. I looked across to see 2 teen gay guys throw at least one trash can through what seemed to be the old Stonewall windows & a lot of chaotic maneuvering & some scrimmaging. The police with lots of vice cops amongst them took on a very vicious fag bashing demeanor. It's clear they planned a fag bashing triumph down on Christopher Street while we were supposed to be off confronting their fag-bashing uptown. Its then we heard people shouting that the women inmates were rioting & throwing out flaming rags. So we all concentrated as support mob for the women inmates. Then the police really got mean as we filled in 6th Av pushing us all into 8th St & filling up 6th Av themselves with different participants & bystanders getting bum-rushed by plainclothesmen out of the crowd then mercilessly beaten then dragged away for arrest. I came to the rescue of one such snatch who for some reason in the blur of the moment seemed to be a fellow 17th St Collective member. My Pink legged foot was on the front page of the New York Times from that moment. I failed but was in turn rescued by Bob Bland. Soon thereafter I was gone for the night & quite fearful of subsequent arrest for several weeks after. I saw what was claimed to be Molotov cocktails getting assembled in a bathtub before the 42nd St Protest, but absolutely no evidence anyone was carrying let alone lighting or tossing any at any time that night.

Ken Lundgreen was a member of the Gay Liberation Front and the 17th Street Collective.

Cover, *The Gay Liberation Movement*, Jack Onge, The Alliance Press, 1971.

"The demonstrators went along Christopher Street and by the time they reached Sheridan Square, their ranks had increased to seven hundred. In Sheridan Square the police were raiding the Haven, a Gay after-hours coffee house, for alcohol and drugs. Law officers used crowbars to tear out phones, furniture, and musical equipment, causing a total of $20,000 in damages. Then police and marchers began shoving each other and a riot broke out, involving one thousand people. Two cars were turned over, and stores selling records and jewelry were robbed."

From *The Gay Liberation Movement*

Martha Shelley

Photo by Steve Rose

GAYS RIOT AGAIN!

REMEMBER THE STONEWALL!

by martha shelley

Once again, the police stepped up their pre-election harassment of Village homosexuals; and once again, we struck back.

For a couple of weeks, police brutality against homosexuals rose to a new high, with beatings and interrogations on the streets of the Village, and a 'clean-up' campaign in the Times Square area which meant over 300 arrests during one week. A young man who was looking at a window display on Times Square was asked by one of New York's Fascists, 'Were you ever arrested?' 'No,' replied the youth. 'There's always a first time,' said the pig, and without being told of any charges, the young man was carted away.

For the first time, women have been hassled by pigs on the streets for being gay—possibly due to the increasing militancy of the Women's Liberation Movement. And so a coalition was formed—Gay Liberation Front, Gay Activists Alliance, Radical Lesbians and various Women's Liberation groups.

Assembling on 42nd Street and Eighth Avenue on Saturday night, August 29th, the groups unfurled their banners and marched several times around 42nd Street, to the amazement of the tourist crowd. We women grouped together in the middle, and to the chants of 'Out of the closets, into the streets!' and 'Gay, gay power to the gay, gay people!', we added, 'Male chauvinist, you better start shakin'—today's pig is tomorrow's bacon!'

After a few turns around the block, the march headed down past the 14th precinct, where it was scheduled to disperse. Since the street was dark and nearly deserted—except for us and some angry pigs—we decided to continue to the Village in order to avoid a battle.

Luck was not with us. On the way down, some straight hoods hurled a couple of bottles at our march, and two of our brothers had to be taken to the hospital with profusely-bleeding scalp wounds. The pig car refused to stop for us, and we had to get there in taxis.

We passed the Women's House of Detention, which inspired the slogan, 'Free our sisters—free ourselves!' The sisters yelled back at us from behind prison bars, 'Power!' When we reached Sheridan Square, the march began to disperse, and we split to go to a party; but suddenly the word filtered back to us: the pigs were raiding the Haven, a gay bar on Sheridan Square. Masses of people, marchers and cruisers, crowded up in front of the Haven. A sister whispered to me, 'There's going to be trouble.' Sure enough, the cops started swinging their nightsticks, and people began to run. Those who had kept their heads began to chant in rhythm, 'Walk.....walk....walk.....'

Word came from behind us that the Women in the House of Detention had begun to riot and to burn their mattresses. We took the crowd back to the House of D. Sure enough, flaming objects were descending from the windows. Some say it was wads of newspaper; some say the sisters had caught rats in their cells and set them afire. We chanted, and they chanted back at us.

The pigs brought on more reinforcements, and our crowd was swelled by Village residents and cruising gay people and local radicals. The pigs moved us off one corner—we took another corner, keeping up the chants. A huge police bus arrived, and a shower of bottles exploded into fragments in front of its headlights—diamonds scattered before swine. Heads were busted. The cops picked up one elderly black man—who knows why—and dragged him into a patrol car. His wife, crying, pleaded for his release. They took her along with him.

The cops pushed us off one corner, and we took another. We took Eighth Street, which had been closed off as a pedestrian mall. I saw some men jumping up on police sawhorses and making speeches, but the words were lost in the roar of the crowd. The battle continued for two or three hours. About a dozen people were arrested.

Some of us stood under the barred windows of the House of D., shouting slogans in English and Spanish. 'Power to the sisters,' we yelled, and they yelled back, 'Power to the gay people!' One lone voice came down, 'I want to be free!'

After midnight, the pigs closed off the pedestrian mall, sweeping the area of people. The rest of us dispersed.

Later, one sister complained to me that as she stood in front of the Haven, some of the people to her rear began to throw bottles at the police, thus provoking a club-swinging melee. Several of the people on the march are of the opinion that agents provocateurs were among us—throwing bottles from the rear while the people up front got clubbed, encouraging acts of violence and vandalism for which others got blamed. In particular, a Volkswagen was overturned. Several GLF'ers have Volkswagens. A record store was looted. Some of our members are self-employed or work in small shops, like record shops and head shops.

There are lessons to be learned from this action. On demonstrations or otherwise, one should never take any action which injures the people, nor should one steal from the people. Agents provocateurs should be surrounded and expelled from the demonstration, just like any germ that enters the bloodstream of a healthy organism. They should be pointed out to other people. Hot-heads should be dissuaded from using a demonstration as an excuse to behave in a manner which injures our cause.

Obviously, pig provocation—as in the increasing number of arrests and beatings of gays, and in the raid on the Haven— must be met with resistance. But our enemies are not anonymous owners of Volkswagens, nor small record shops.

On the whole, the demonstration was a success, both in terms of the increasing pride among members of the gay community and in the increasing support we are getting from Women's Liberation, the sisters in the House of D., and other members of the radical community. We're getting it together, and the pigs can't stop us now!

Come Out!, Vol. 1, No. 5, September-October 1970.

Gays Riot Again! Remember the Stonewall

Once again, the police stepped up their pre-election harassment of Village homosexuals; and once again, we struck back.

For a couple of weeks police brutality against homosexuals rose to a new high, with beatings and interrogations on the streets of the Village, and a 'clean-up' campaign in the Times Square are which meant over 300 arrests during one week. A young man who was looking at a window display on Times Square was asked by one of New York's Fascists, "Were you ever arrested?" "No," replied the youth. "There's always a first time," said the pig, and without being told of any charges, the young man was carried away.

For the first time women have been hassled by pigs on the street for being gay—possibly due to the increasing militancy of the Women's Liberation Movement. And so a coalition was formed—Gay Liberation Front, Gay Activists Alliance, Radical Lesbians and various Women's Liberation groups.

Assembling on 42nd Street and Eighth Avenue on Saturday night, August 29th, the groups unfurled their banners and marched several times around 42nd Street, to the amazement of the tourist crowd. We women grouped together in the middle, and to the chants of "Out of the closets, into the streets!" and Gay, gay power to the gay, gay people!" we added, "Male chauvinist you better start shakin'—today's pig is tomorrow's bacon."

After a few turns around the block, the march headed down past the 14th precinct, where it was scheduled to disperse. Since the street was dark and nearly deserted—except for us and some angry pigs—we decided to continue to the Village in order to avoid a battle.

Luck was not with us. On the way down, some straight hoods hurled a couple of bottles at our march, and two of our brothers had to be taken to the hospital with profusely-bleeding scalp wounds. The pig car refused to stop for us, and we had to get there in taxis. We passed the Women's House of Detention, which inspired the slogan, "Free our sisters—free ourselves. The sisters yelled back at us from behind prison bars. "Power!" When we reached Sheridan Square, the march began to disperse, and we split to go to a party; but suddenly the word filtered back to us: the pigs were raiding the Haven, a gay bar on Sheridan Square. Masses of people, marchers and cruisers, crowded up in front of the Haven. As sister whispered to me, "There's going to be trouble." Sure enough, the cops started swinging their nightsticks, and people began to run. Those who had kept their heads began to chant in rhythm, "Walk...walk... walk..."

Word cam from behind us that the women in the House of Detention had begun to riot and to burn their mattresses. We took the crowd back to the House of D. Sure enough, flaming objects were descending from the windows. Some say it was wads of newspaper, some say the sisters had caught rats in their cells and set them afire. We chanted, and they chanted back at us.

The pigs brought on more reinforcements, and our crowd was swelled by Village residents and cruising gay people and local radicals. The pigs moved us off one corner—we took another corner, keeping up the chants. A huge police bus arrived, and a shower of bottles exploded into fragments in front of its headlights—diamonds scattered before swine. Heads were busted. The cops picked up one elderly black man—who knows why—and dragged him into a patrol car. His wife, crying, pleaded for his release. They took her along with him.

The cops pushed us off one corner, and we took another. We took Eighth Street, which had been closed off as a pedestrian mall. I saw some men jumping up on police sawhorses and making speeches, but the words were lost in the roar of the crowd. The battle continued for two or three hours. About a dozen people were arrested.

Some of us stood under the barred windows of the House of D, shouting slogans in English and Spanish. "Power to the sisters," we yelled, and they yelled back, "Power to the gay people!" One lone voice came down, "I want to be free!" After midnight the pigs closed off the pedestrian mall, sweeping the area of people. The rest of us dispersed.

Later, one sister complained to me that as she stood in from of the Haven, some of the people to her rear began to throw bottles at the police, this provoking a club-swinging melee. Several of the on the march are of the opinion that agents provocateurs were among us—throwing bottles from the rear while the people up front got clubbed, encouraging acts of violence and vandalism for which others got blamed. In particular, a Volkswagen was overturned. Several GLFers have Volkswagens. A record store was looted. Some of our members are self-employed or work in small shops, like record shops and head shops.

There are lessons to be learned from this action. On demonstrations or otherwise, one should never take any action which injures the people, nor should one steal from the people. Agents provocateurs should be surrounded and expelled from the demonstration, just like any germ that enters the bloodstream of a healthy organism. They should be pointed out to other people. Hot-heads should be dissuaded from using a demonstration as an excuse to behave in a manner which injures our cause.

Obviously, pig provocation—as in the increasing number of arrests and beatings of gays, and in the raid on the Haven—must be me with resistance. Bur our enemies are not anonymous owners of Volkswagens, nor small record shops.

On the whole, the demonstration was a success, both in terms of the increasing pride among members of the gay community and in the increasing support we are getting from Women's Liberation, the sisters of the House of D, and other members of the radical community. We're getting it together, and the pigs can't stop us now!

Postscript

If I were writing the article today, I wouldn't use the term pigs to describe the police, or copy other parts of the Black Panther (or any other leftist) rhetoric. It is a substitute for intelligent thought and good writing. It turns off the people we want to reach, just like overturning a Volkswagen or vandalizing a small business turns them off. A simple description of events is more powerful. That said, the police don't seem to have changed much. They can occasionally be heroic, for example on 9/11. They stood up for the unions and against Gov. Walker in Wisconsin recently-- remarkably enough, because their stance was so unusual. They have been and continue to be employed on behalf of the monied elite rather than the ordinary citizens whose taxes pay their salaries. The Occupy movement is only the latest target.

Portland, 2012

Martha Shelley was one of the founders of GLF-New York and of Radicalesbians. She also worked on RAT Newspaper and the Women's Press Collective (Oakland), and produced the nation's first lesbian radio show for WBAI-FM. Her most recent work is a novel, *The Throne in the Heart of the Sea*.

Photograph © copyright 1970 by Steve Rose.

Dennis Siple

I can't recall the first part of the demonstration and the march downtown. I know that at some point we were herded off of Christopher Street and across Sixth Avenue, onto Eighth Street, after a scuffle with the cops. Someone had been wounded by a blow to the head and his blood was in the street. Hank bent down and put his hand in the pool of blood and climbed up on a lamppost so he could be seen, raised his hand high and screamed, "This is the blood of your brother!" In that moment, skinny little Hank became huge; fierce! Of all of my time in GLF, of all the demonstrations I screamed and made noises at, I can't remember an image that seared itself so hotly on my brain. That is to me, the iconic moment, the commemorative postage stamp of our Revolution.

Dennis Siple began his activism with GLF in 1970. Living from the start of the epidemic, he's been involved with Queer Nation, Act Up, and the AIDS Mastery. He served on the Board of Hollywood Community Housing Corporation, a developer of HIV/AIDS housing for 14 years.

Rich Wandel

The beginning of all that came after . . .

The summer of 1970 was the beginning of everything. Maybe not the absolute beginning. I witnessed with my generation three assassinations, watched the police riot in 1968 Chicago, campaigned for the poor of Biafra, and tutored neglected children in Hartford's North End. But this was new, more personal. I came out to myself at the age of 24, late by today's standards, but not unusual for a Catholic ex-seminarian in 1970. In August of that year I went to see some friends at the monastery I was last in, St. Michael's, Union City, New Jersey, just across the Hudson from New York City. My way home took me through Times Square from the Port Authority at 8th Avenue through to the 6th Avenue subway a few blocks away. I came upon a demonstration in progress. I had known of the demonstration before-hand but was not consciously planning on attending—a bit afraid I suppose.

It's hard to remember; events become conflated. I joined in the crowd of fifty or so people circling the blocks between 7th and 8th Avenues to protest the latest round of "cleaning up" Times Square, an election-year tradition that swept up in its net anyone the police thought looked gay. Gay Liberation Front (GLF) and Gay Activists Alliance (GAA) joined together in protest. Very low-key by later standards, but yet an all but unheard of public gathering of angry, politically minded gays. Many marchers had handmade signs marching along with the larger banners of GLF and of GAA, and an even larger banner of Youth Against War and Fascism (YAWF). YAWF and their banner were at any kind of demonstration. We made several circuits up and down 42nd Street, staying on the sidewalk like nice law-abiding demonstrators, waving signs and chanting at the amused passersby.

In the summer of 1970 gays were still considered powerless and for that reason we were mildly amusing. After a while, someone made the decision to move the demonstration to the police precinct that was responsible for carrying out the harassment on Times Square. The group headed south past the offending police station and then continued on to Greenwich Village.

The Women's House of Detention, a New York City prison long protested by New York's radical left for its poor condition and treatment of female inmates, took up most of a small triangle of land bordered by 6th Avenue, Greenwich Avenue and West 10th Street. We began to circle it, round-and-round like Joshua at Jericho. From windows high above, the women inmates called out to us, cheered, and lit bits of paper which they tossed out the windows, points of light floating down to Greenwich Avenue, acknowledging the demonstrators and declaring solidarity with us.

GAA's constitution required it to involve the organization in only specifically gay and lesbian issues, although most of its members had a consciousness that took in a wider political understanding. The GAA banner was folded and put away, but many of its members, including myself, remained. When we arrived at 6th Avenue and 8th Street, we discovered that 8th Street had been closed to traffic for the evening, creating a pedestrian mall slated to continue until midnight. We danced in the street. More and more people, mostly young like me, joined in the dance. It was exhilarating to be gay, open, and celebratory. Eventually midnight arrived, the time for the street to reopen to traffic. We continued dancing. The police ordered us to leave, but we continued the celebration.

The police gathered at the edge of the crowd on 6th avenue, joined by the baby-blue-helmeted officers of the Tactical Patrol Force—an elite riot police. I was both afraid and fascinated. I had some idea of the possibilities—I had seen police violence on TV. I couldn't leave; I couldn't stay. I danced, keeping back from the frontline on 6th Avenue. Memories get confused as I retell a story told many times—my own personal mythmaking, my crossing the threshold into the gay movement. I remember dancing in sandaled feet with others in a sort of snake dance until one of my sandals broke. I remember being told that someone was throwing things at the police, arching their missiles from within the crowd and over the frontline of demonstrators. I remember the police in response arbitrarily choosing some smallish person in the front and clubbing him.

Fear overcame fascination. I took my broken sandal and went home to Brooklyn, but I had "seen" blood on the streets and become part of a community I had only theoretically been connected with before. The foundational event: a turning point, the beginning of all that came after, an important realization, made me part of a community.

Rich Wandel was the second president of New York's Gay Activists Alliance (GAA) and is the founder and current archivist/ historian of New York's LGBT Community Center's National History Archive.

I was there all the way.

Tom Ashe

The News photographer, noting that I was wearing anti-teargas goggles, at that moment dangling from my neck, made sure to click on me. This was just north of the intersection of 8th Street and 6th Avenue. Only a moment before, we had all sat down in that intersection and 'liberated' it. Martha Shelley happened to be sitting next to me. "Isn't this wonderful?" she exulted, with which I agreed vociferously.

Kenneth Pitchford

I remember we marched to protest harassment of hustlers and street people from the 42nd area, heading downtown, chanting "out of the showers and into the streets" when we passed the YMCA.

Allen Young

Self-Portrait 2010

Steven F. Dansky, publisher of Christopher Street Press, has been an activist, photographer, and writer for more than fifty years. He was a founder of the Effeminist Movement and an original member of Gay Liberation Front.

www.ingramcontent.com/pod-product-compliance
Lightning Source LLC
Chambersburg PA
CBHW061510040426
42450CB00008B/1556